IMAGES OF ENGLAND

THE MALVERNS

IMAGES OF ENGLAND

THE MALVERNS

BRIAN ILES

TEMPUS

Frontispiece: A Francis Bedford image of Belle Vue Terrace in Great Malvern, *c.* 1860.

First published 2005

Tempus Publishing Limited
The Mill, Brimscombe Port,
Stroud, Gloucestershire, GL5 2QG
www.tempus-publishing.com

British Library Cataloguing in Publication Data.
A catalogue record for this book is available from the British Library.

ISBN 0 7524 3667 8

Typesetting and origination by Tempus Publishing Limited.
Printed in Great Britain.

Contents

Acknowledgements

Most of the illustrations in this book are from my own collection of local photographs and postcards amassed over the last thirty or so years. Apart from collecting anything connected with the history of the Malverns and the surrounding area, I also help run Malvern Museum and have included some pictures from their collection, for which I am very grateful. I also acknowledge the loan of photographs by the following: Howard Stanley, Gwyn Nicholls, Trevor Sadler, Richard Manning, Isobel Stanley and Shirley Iles. I would also like to thank Keith Smith, who originally made the suggestion that I produce this book and recommended me to Tempus.

Most of all I heartily thank all those photographers of the past, without whom this book would not have been possible. These include national photographers such as Francis Bedford and John Latham plus local photographers, including Clem Walton, Norman May, T. Bennett & Sons, Francis Earl, C. & E. Grosvenor, A.H. Robbins, William Bushnell, John Downs, J. Shambrook, Tilley & Son and all of the anonymous local cameramen throughout the ages, from the very earliest days of photography.

Introduction

The Malverns have been inhabited since at least the Iron Age, notably around two sites on the hills, the British Camp and Midsummer Hill. At that time, it would have been a largely rural area, the locals having been mostly farmers, growing crops for themselves and even exporting their surplus. During the Norman period, much of the lands on and around the hills were set up as a royal hunting forest, Malvern Chase.

After the eleventh century, the town would have centred on the two Benedictine priories at Great Malvern and Little Malvern. Malvern Priory, the Priory Gatehouse and part of Little Malvern Priory survive today, although the timber Guesten Hall was unfortunately demolished in the nineteenth century.

For centuries, Malvern water has been famed for its healing properties and the Victorian era saw the growth of water-cure establishments, run by doctors like Gully, Wilson and Grindrod. They attracted many visitors, including famous personalities such as Charles Dickens, Alfred Lord Tennyson, Florence Nightingale and Charles Darwin, who were all searching for a cure for their ailments. Patients would have various water treatments coupled with exercise; they would be sent to 'take the waters' at the various springs and sprouts around the hills. Malvern water has been bottled and sold for many years by local companies such as Burrows, Cuffs, Berkeleys, Ballards, Bennetts, Lewis, Allens, Boormans, Simpson & Cross, Jones & Davis and the Royal Well. It has latterly been bottled by Schweppes and today by Coca Cola Enterprises. Malvern water is even favoured by HM the Queen.

During the nineteenth century, the town and surrounding areas began to expand. In 1800 the population of Malvern was less than 1,000. By 1855 there were ninety-five hotel and lodging house keepers; ten years later their numbers had increased to 200, which was about 25 per cent of the households in Malvern.

The nineteenth century, following the Malvern Hills Act in 1844, saw the birth of the Malvern Hills Conservators, who continue to administer and protect the hills and commons today. Much of the lands and properties in the Malvern area were once owned and controlled by several family estates, including the Foleys, Hornyolds and

Beauchamps, who played a significant part in the Victorian development of Malvern. However, over the twentieth century much of their lands have been sold off.

Malvern was a popular spot to enjoy holidays, evidenced by the many postcards and souvenirs of the late Victorian and Edwardian periods that still exist today. The hills and commons are still popular for outdoor pursuits like rambling and hang-gliding.

Malvern produced one of the earliest motor cars in the world, the Santler Malvernia, which is still in existence. It has also long been the home of the famous Morgan sports car, still produced at the Pickersleigh Road factory and exported to aficionados all over the world.

Private schools were being established in Malvern in the Victorian era, some of which survive today. These include Malvern College, Malvern Girls' College and St James and the Abbey.

The period from 1929 through the 1930s was the heyday of the Malvern film and theatre festivals, at which Edward Elgar and George Bernard Shaw were much in evidence, as were their musical and dramatic works. Actors like Errol Flynn, Stewart Grainger, Wendy Hiller, Robert Donat and Ernest Thesinger could often be seen in the streets between plays. Edward Elgar lived for many years in Malvern and is buried at St Wulstan's church. The present theatres still attract famous performers and many visitors today.

The Second World War saw an influx of American soldiers and nurses at the five army hospitals in the Malvern area, which supplied 10,000 beds for the war-wounded. There were also Belgians, Canadians, Poles and Free French present in the town. The Royal Navy had a training establishment, HMS *Duke*, based here and the redundant railway tunnel was used to store torpedoes.

The Telecommunications Research Establishment (TRE) was evacuated to Malvern during the war and radar was developed here, the success of which played no small part in bringing the war to an end, prompting the comment; 'Waterloo was won on the playing fields of Eton but the Second World War was won on the playing fields of Malvern'. The scientific establishment remained after the war and many significant developments, particularly those connected with radar and crystal sciences, have originated here. It operates today as QuinetiQ and is still a major employer in the area.

I hope that the pictures and information in this book will evoke memories in those who, like myself, live in and love Malvern and those who have lived or worked here in the past. The book will perhaps inspire others to record their memories for like-minded people in the future.

I make no apologies for advertising here Malvern Museum, which is entirely run by local volunteers and is always grateful for the donation or loan of local material to add to its records of Malvern's past for the benefit of people today and people of the future. The museum always has a need for new volunteers to help keep it open for the people of Malvern and its visitors.

Brian Iles
May 2005

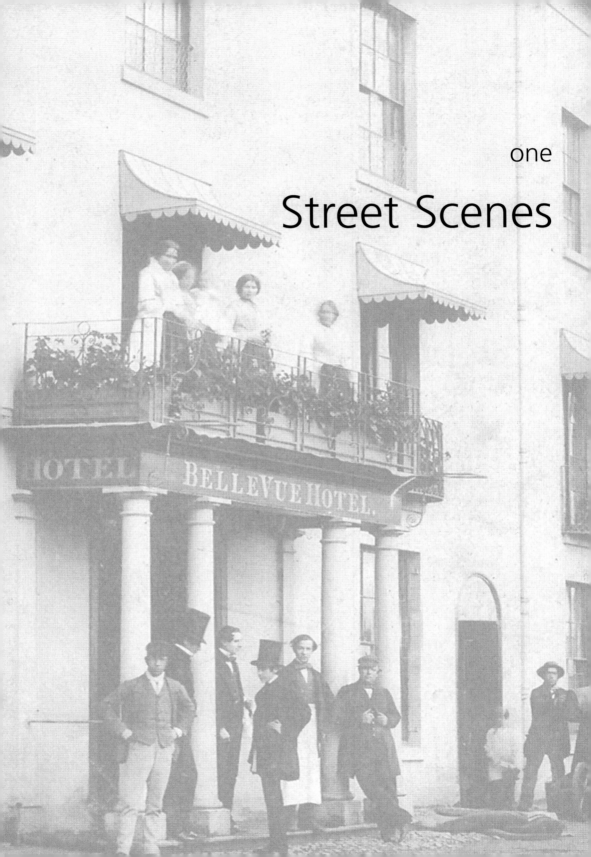

one

Street Scenes

An early photograph from the 1860s, showing the now demolished vicarage in Abbey Road. This site is presently occupied by the general post office.

The top of Church Street, *c.* 1865. The row of shops on the right was then known as Paradise Row. The three-wheeled carriage could be hired and would have been either pulled by a pony or donkey or even pushed by hand – not an easy job up and down Malvern's steep hills.

Above: The Belle Vue Hotel on Belle Vue Terrace in the 1860s. The buildings have since had shopfronts added at ground floor level. The colonnaded building in the distance was the Royal Library, which today is a bank. The number of people who have gathered suggests that the photographer has created a lot of interest; the camera would have been very high-tech in its day. The man with the wheeled barrel, to the right of the hotel porch, may have been collecting night soil or kitchen leftovers for pig swill.

Right: This is the other end of Belle Vue Terrace, showing the shop and post office of Henry Cross, who published this photograph. Cross also operated a branch of Mudie's Select Library from the premises, as well as a bookshop, printer's and stationer's.

The southern end of Belle Vue Terrace in the 1870s. The four-wheeled carriage, which is being pulled by a pony, would have been for hire like the three-wheeled carriage seen earlier.

A later view of the location shown in the photograph above, Belle Vue Terrace, taken in 1911. The motor car, which has an early local AB registration, appears to be struggling up the incline. The lady cyclist just about to descend the hill must have had great faith in the brakes of her bicycle.

Belle Vue Terrace, *c.* 1925. The first doorway on the left led to the Oak Room and the shops included Crighton's Outfitters and Achille Sorre. The ornate hotel porch of the Belle Vue Hotel has now disappeared. The motor charabanc parked on the right is picking up passengers for its next trip.

The junction of Belle Vue Terrace, Worcester Road and the top of Church Street in Great Malvern, *c.* 1925. The WHSmith shop is still in the same location, on the site previously occupied by the premises of Henry Cross. Next door was Morley's confectionery shop – Mr Morley had perished in the *Titanic* disaster in 1912 – and Woodyatt's garage. In the middle distance can be seen the White Horse Hotel and the Malvern Dairy shop. One of the shops on the right, by the parked motorcycle combination, was the hairdresser's establishment of H. Burley, which is still in business today and is run by a descendant of the same family.

Rose Bank, Great Malvern, 1911. Sadly, the house has since been demolished, although the gardens still exist.

The top of Church Street, with the northern end of Belle Vue Terrace and Worcester Road beyond. The cart descending the hill appears to be in the charge of a young boy. The heavily laden cart at the top of the hill is negotiating a tight turn into Church Street.

Above: The top of Great Malvern, taken from the tower of Malvern Priory in the 1880s. In the centre foreground can be seen the rear of the old vicarage and beyond, in Church Street, are the shops of Paradise Row. Below this part of Church Street, the houses still have their gardens, as this was before the construction of the present-day shops.

Right: The southern elevation of the Priory Gatehouse. It looks much the same today, although the weathercock has since disappeared. Note the ice-cream vendor with his cart in the bottom right-hand corner.

The northern elevation of the Priory Gatehouse, 1910. This was taken after its reconstruction in the 1890s. The building is now the home of Malvern Museum.

Abbey Road, from the top of the priory tower. The premises of Warwick House, occupied by Cox & Painter, have yet to be extended. The Hay Well buildings in the centre of the photograph, which have since been replaced by a church, have not yet been demolished.

Looking up Church Street from just below the crossroads. The building on the left, behind the flagpole, was occupied by Sharpe's ironmongers and a livery stable (on a site now occupied by a bank and Woolworths). Baylis the chemist, on the right-hand side of the road, had his own advertising street lamp.

St Ann's Road, looking up from just above the Unicorn, 1911. At the top are Welch's Dining Rooms. The Central Hotel and other premises catered for the cyclist.

A horse-drawn charabanc waiting outside the Lygon Arms at Link Top, Malvern. The bunting on the buildings indicates that this was taken during a royal occasion, probably either the Diamond Jubilee of Queen Victoria in 1897 or the Coronation of King George V in 1911.

Worcester Road, Malvern Link in the 1930s. The Co-operative shop still occupies the same site today. The 'No Waiting' signs permit parking on each side of the road on alternate days, although the parked vehicles indicate that the drivers of the day did not take a lot of notice of the regulations.

Malvern Link, looking eastwards down Worcester Road. Colston Buildings, on the left, housed shops such as WHSmith and Rhodes' China Stores. On the right were the Railway Inn, J. Hawkins' confectioners, S.L. Wade's caterers and bakers, and the Bakery Inn. Further down was the Fir Tree Inn.

Malvern Link, looking westwards from further down Worcester Road. On the left, at the crossroads, was Boorman's chemists, who sold Malvern Hygienic Waters. On the right were E.F. Swaffield's tailors and outfitters and the premises of Santler, motor engineer and garage proprietor. Santler not only built bicycles but had previously built the Malvernia, one of the first ever motor cars.

An early view looking up towards the hills and Great Malvern from the tower of the Imperial Hotel, now Malvern Girls' College. Imperial and Avenue Roads in the foreground had a distinct lack of buildings at that time.

Barnards Green, from the traffic island, in 1918. Shops included Badham's saddlers, F.S. Ranford's garage, E. Thaley's confectioners and stationers, and Smith's of London house outfitters, hosiers and hatters.

Barnards Green, seen from the other end of the island, *c.* 1920. The horse trough has since been relocated to the Hall Green junction with Guarlford Road.

Barnards Green, looking towards Guarlford Road, *c.* 1900.

Malvern Wells, 1911. The supply stores on the right was also a Midland Railway parcel receiving office.

The Hornyold Arms Hotel at Malvern Wells after a heavy snowfall in 1918.

two

Work, Trade and Industry

The interior of Cox & Painter's shop at Warwick House in Great Malvern, *c.* 1910.

The ladies' department of Warwick House, *c.* 1910.

Above: Lewis & Son's Café Royal at the junction of the top of Edith Walk and Church Street. The building has since been replaced by a bank.

Right: Edward Archer's wine shop and Harper & Son estate agents were situated in the buildings of the previous Coburg Baths, which were designed by Samuel Deykes.

Left: Gwynn & Sons in Church Street, *c.* 1910. There are still items of furniture made by this company in existence today.

Below: The interior of Gwynn & Sons' shop.

Cridlan & Walker's butchers in Abbey Road, *c.* 1900. This photograph was taken by local photographer Norman May. Note the steels hanging from the butchers' belts, always at the ready to keep their knives sharp.

Rhodes' China and Glass Depot on the Promenade in Worcester Road, Great Malvern. Rhodes also had another shop in Colston Buildings, Malvern Link.

Thirwall & Thornton's drapers at Orleans House in Church Street, Great Malvern.

Malvern had many chemist shops and pharmacies. This was the interior of Armstrong's in Great Malvern.

Opposite above: A.S. Clarke's chemist shop in Church Street.

Opposite below: The stationery and fancy goods shop of Henry Guy at Paris House in Church Street. This shop later became Cameron's before they moved to other premises lower down Church Street.

Mander's Belle Vue pharmacy on Belle Vue Terrace, complete with its decorative carboys in the windows.

The premises of J. Nott, tea dealer and provision merchant, in Church Street, *c.* 1910.

Opposite above: Kendall's department store and the Beauchamp Hotel, at the Church Street and Graham Road crossroads, *c.* 1880.

Opposite below: The piano repair workshop of Oxley's in Church Street.

Left: Many of the photographs of local events, people and buildings taken by T. Bennett & Sons survive today. This was their shop at Gazebo House in Church Street.

Below: George Smith's Promenade Restaurant in Worcester Road, Great Malvern. The restaurant is now an antique shop.

Right: George Smith also operated a bakery in Newtown Road. The premises still operate as a bakery to this day.

Below: An interior view of Smith's bakery, with plenty of freshly baked bread and what looks like pies being made in the left foreground.

Link Top, *c.* 1912. At the top of Lygon Bank are East's saddlery premises. They also sold Firkin's gloves, which were made in Worcester. Next door is Edward Bury & Co., basketmakers and newsagents. Along the road are the Lygon Arms, selling Allen Bros beers from the Brompton Brewery in Newtown Road, the Lygon Pharmacy, Isaac's family drapers, Howell & Stevens' grocers, W. & A. Gilbey's wine merchants and the Vaults public house.

Edward Bury's shop, 1931. A wide range of goods is on display. The shop has since been extended forwards to cover the area under the canopy.

Above and below: Howell & Stevens' grocery shop at Link Top. On the right of the picture below, there are many large tins of loose biscuits; often these tins would have glass lids to enable the contents to be easily seen. There was frequently one at the end containing broken biscuits, which were usually popular with children.

The Nag's Head at the bottom of Bank Street. This public house would have been popular with visitors to Link Common and the fairgrounds sited there during bank holidays. The building on the right, on what is now the car park, was the photographic studio of William Bushnell, who took this photograph.

F.A. Bubb's greengrocery at Link Top. The shop's specialities were the locally produced Malvoma tomatoes and cucumbers. Malvoma had extensive greenhouses in Pickersleigh Road. They seem to have had a record early crop in this year, producing tomatoes on 31 March. This is nothing special today but at that time most produce was seasonable and locally grown. The Link Top public water supply pump can be seen behind the boy on the left.

The Newtown Furniture Stores of C. Hayes, at the junction of Queens Road and Newtown Road, next to A. Wigley's drapers, clothiers, post office, tobacconists and stationers.

An early photograph of Cook & Casson's carriage and harness manufacturers in Spring Lane, Malvern Link. The premises were on the site of what is now a supermarket car park.

Russell's butchers in Worcester Road, Malvern Link, decorated for the Diamond Jubilee of Queen Victoria in 1897. The photograph was taken by C. & E. Grosvenor. The butchers have their sharpening steels hanging ready for use on their belts. Note the ox tongues hanging above the man in the doorway.

A delivery cart belonging to Russell's butchers standing outside Cole's Chase Coachworks in Upper Chase Road. The sign says 'Winners of five first and special prizes'.

The shop of Towndrow & Holbrook at Malvern Wells, next to the Wells Institute. They appear to have photographs and picture postcards for sale in the window.

Holbrook and Adams' shop in West Malvern Road.

The Holy Well at Malvern Wells. Schweppes first bottled Malvern water at this site before moving to Colwall, after which Cuffs took over and also bottled water and produced soft drinks. Schweppes built a copy of this building at their new Colwall bottling works.

Malvern water and soft drinks were bottled and beer brewed at the Royal Well at Upper Colwall. This late nineteenth-century photograph shows well workers posing by the roadside well-spout. There was, for a short time, a concert hall on the adjacent site, at which international singing star Jenny Lind, the Swedish Nightingale, made her very last public performance.

The Priory Gatehouse is not usually considered to be a shop but it was at one time used as an outlet for game produce, vegetables and so on, in this case by E. Clay. Items such as rabbits would have been displayed on the rail to the right of the archway.

This stand advertised Malvern and its produce at a trade exhibition. Trade exhibitions used to be held in Lowesmore, Worcester and it is possible that this photograph was taken there.

This horse–drawn delivery cart belonged to J. Corbett of Poolbrook, a grocer and baker.

A.J. Bird's delivery horse and cart. His shop was in Barnards Green.

Haymaking at Cygnet Farm, Hanley Swan in 1912. The man with the shotgun probably bagged any rabbits that ran away as reaping progressed.

Making hay while the sun shines, with Malvern Wells and the Malvern Hills in the background. The haymakers are all wearing hats or bonnets to protect their heads.

There used to be stone quarries all around the hills and surrounding area. This quarry at North Malvern was operated by Pyx and Malvern Urban District Council. The clock tower contained the local water supply spout, which was fed from the tanks behind.

Quarrying at Winds Point, by the British Camp. Prior to the advent of motor transport, the stone would all have been transported by horse and cart.

The Wilson brickworks at Belmont, off Cowleigh Bank, looking down from North Malvern. Many buildings in Malvern were built using local Wilson's bricks.

A local cider apple press. The photograph was taken by local photographer Clem Walton.

Left: There would have been many people employed as carters to transport goods, materials and people in, out and around the district. Extra horses would have been stationed at strategic points to assist in hauling heavy loads up the many steep hills and roads of Malvern. This cart has just been pulled up to the Wyche Cutting.

Below: To service all of the horses, ponies, donkeys and associated equipment, there would have been many farriers and blacksmiths in the area. This one was at nearby Leigh Sinton.

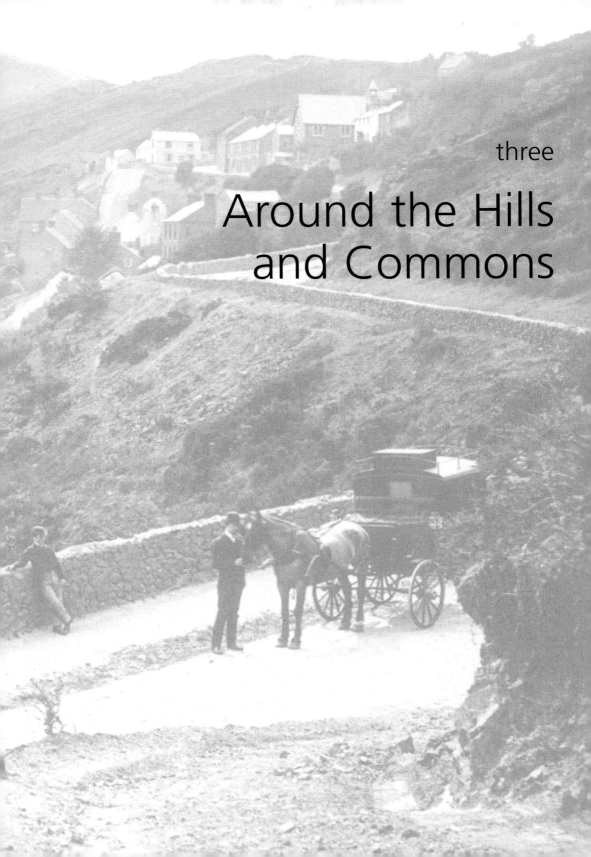

three

Around the Hills and Commons

Left: A Malvern Hills donkey and its passengers, *c.* 1880. The photograph was taken by Francis Earl. Presumably one paid a cheaper fare if the poor donkey carried three children at once.

Below: Wyche Cutting, *c.* 1880. The young boy is taking a rest with his yoke and two pails. He would have been most likely fetching water from the nearby public spout.

Wyche Road under construction, in a photograph by Francis Bedford. The coach belonged to Bedford and it often appears in his pictures. Its raised roof presumably allowed him to stand inside to process his photographic plates. The boxes piled by the wall would have been for his camera equipment.

Donkeys awaiting customers in 1911. Most of the donkeys are fitted with side-saddles so that they could be ridden by women. The message on the rear of this postcard is from John and Phoebe Wilcox and says, 'Dear sister, we went to Malvern on Monday and never enjoyed ourselves better'.

Left: A view across St Ann's Well, showing John Down's camera obscura in the distance on St Ann's Delight.

Below: John Down's camera obscura. The view was reflected down by the mirror on the roof to a dish-shaped table inside the building. The mirror could be rotated to show a panoramic moving view of the surrounding hills and beyond.

The camera obscura was at one time installed on the Worcestershire Beacon in this stone building known locally as Downs Castle. The mirror can be seen on the building on the left. The entrance fee was 3¼d.

The stone buildings were later replaced by these timber ones, with the obscura mirror on the right-hand roof. The building on the left was a tea room.

A very early photograph of St Ann's Well, taken in the 1850s. The men seated on the left are possibly the German or Berlin band that performed in the Malvern area at the time.

The tea gardens at St Ann's Well, complete with their Coalbrookdale cast-iron fern pattern benches.

St Ann's Well after the construction of the polygonal extension, in a photograph taken by Francis Bedford. A donkey cart has just arrived with its passenger, who has no doubt come to take the waters.

Ivy Scar Rock with a fence and kissing gate across the path. The photographer has left a spare camera and tripod by the seat underneath the rock face.

An early photograph looking down Happy Valley before it was planted with trees. Note the buildings on top of the hill to the right, which may have been houses for local workers.

Victorian walkers taking a well-earned rest. It must have been hot and tiring climbing the hills in the heavy dress of the period.

A view across Link Common towards the hills. The fields to the left have since had houses built on them, including Meadow Road and Cedar Avenue.

Cockshot Pond on the common at Link Top, 1916. Moorlands Road is on the left and Graham Road at the top. This pond was full of pond life and was popular with local children, who fished for sticklebacks and tadpoles.

The British Camp Hotel and Wynds Point Quarry in an early photograph by Francis Bedford. A house later built in the quarry became the home of famous singer Jenny Lind, the Swedish Nightingale.

The British Camp, 1920s. The amount of traffic indicates that it was probably taken during a motor club outing or on a bank holiday. There is a group of bull-nose Morris cars on the right-hand side and several motor charabancs in the car park.

four

Sport

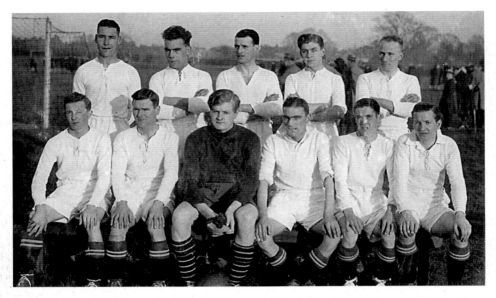

Barnards Green football team in the 1936/37 season. From left to right, back row: Bill Mann, Len Lewis, Rob Cullen, J. Hodgkins, Tom Brant. Front row: John McCary, Bert Amphlett, Richard 'Dickie' Lygon, Bob Harding, Billy McCary, Arthur Brown.

Malvern Link Football Club in the 1919/20 season. The photograph was taken by C. & E. Grosvenor.

Opposite above: Quest Hills Football Club in the 1910/11 season.

Opposite below: Poolbrook Youth Club football team in 1948. From left to right, back row: R. Meek, A. Moore, Revd Mayne, J. Passey, H. Stanley, D. Young, A. Holt, –?–, Revd Iverson, H. Smart, ? Summers. Middle row: R. Young, R. Gittings, J. Snee, G. Wardroper, A. Smith. Front row: J. White, G. White, A. Davies.

The tennis courts at Manor Park, with Lansdowne Road Hospital in the background.

Croquet players and officials at Manor Park during a tournament in 1909.

Opposite above: Wimbledon ladies' tennis champion Dorothy Round (holding the book) at Manor Park in 1935.

Opposite below: West Malvern cricket team, 1909, in a photograph by Grosvenor.

The swimming baths at St Cuthbert's, Malvern Link.

The British Camp Hotel swimming pool, *c.* 1930. The pool was situated on the opposite side of Jubilee Drive from the hotel.

The public swimming baths at Priory Park in Great Malvern, *c.* 1920. They still looked much the same forty years later but have since been replaced by the Splash complex.

An aerial view of Colwall Park racecourse, which is now no longer in existence.

One of the men in this group at the Malvern Link Golf Club is six times open champion Harry Vardon.

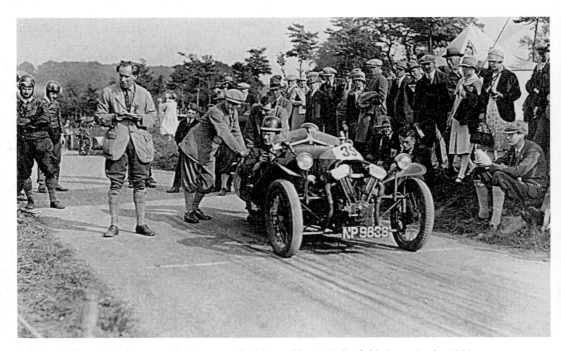

A Morgan three-wheeler competing in a speed trial, possibly at Madresfield Court, in the 1920s.

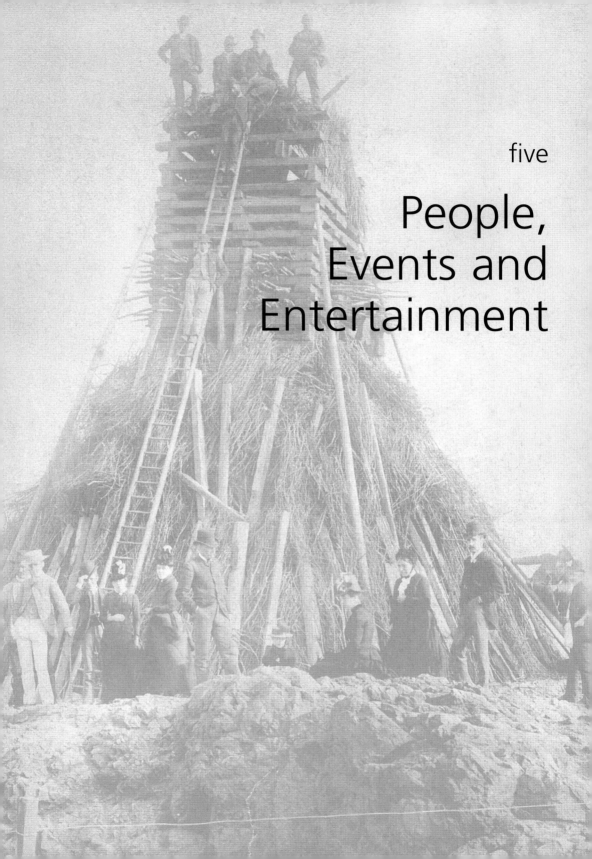

five

People, Events and Entertainment

Above: A Malvern theatre festival garden party. These parties were as much part of the local scene as were the festival performances. The tall man in the centre of this group is Stewart Grainger, who played at Malvern twice in the 1930s. He was known as James Stewart in 1936 but had changed his name to Stewart Grainger when he appeared at the festival in 1937.

Left: Robert Donat walking along Abbey Road. Donat appeared in festival plays in 1933 and 1935.

Opposite above: Roy Limbert (with bow tie) and J.B. Priestley (on the right, smoking a pipe) during the 1938 festival. Priestley gave a talk at the festival that year.

Opposite below: This group on the Winter Gardens Terrace includes Roy Limbert and actress Wendy Hiller, who famously played Eliza Doolittle in Shaw's *Pygmalion* both on the Malvern Theatre stage and in the film version.

Left: George Bernard Shaw at a garden party in the grounds of the County Hotel in Abbey Road.

Below: Gillian Lind and Isobel Thornton taking the waters at the Jacob Fountain in the Winter Gardens in 1931. Isobel Thornton appeared at Malvern in many of the pre-war festivals.

Local artist Illingworth Varley and family with their goat cart, during the Coronation festivities of 1911.

Rose Bank Gardens, 1932. Everybody seems to be enjoying the band's performance, with the exception of the little girl in the foreground, who is intent on playing with her doll's pram.

Alfred Toones Band, posed in front of the bandstand at Rose Bank.

Malvern Improvement Association Band. All but two of the band members are sporting
moustaches. The Association also produced publicity material and Malvern guides.

West Malvern Brass Band.

A Clem Walton photograph of a Malvern Wells band. Some of the players seem to be holding rather strange home-made musical instruments.

A local choir at a Madresfield musical competition. These ladies won the banner and first prize in 1912.

E. Smith of North Malvern took this photograph of children trying to eat apples hanging on strings. It was presumably taken at a local fête in around 1911, possibly during the Coronation festivities.

An encampment of gypsies in Cradley for the hop-picking in 1910.

Opposite below: A photograph of a local wedding, taken by William Bushnell of Bank Street in 1910. Mr Bushnell had a unique way of posing his subjects in this picture: some are sitting on the ground and others are standing on chairs.

A large crowd on the common at Link Top, by the junction of Moorlands Road and Worcester Road, during the Coronation festivities in 1911.

HRH the Duchess of York at Great Malvern in 1934. Local Girl Guides are providing a guard of honour.

Above: The Coronation bonfire on the Worcestershire Beacon in 1911. This was quite a large structure and the men perched on top must have had a lot of confidence in the stability of their bonfire.

Right: An earlier bonfire on the Beacon, celebrating the Golden Jubilee of Queen Victoria in 1887.

Left: The Malvern Hills have always been a popular tobogganing spot for adults and children alike. This group are coming down Happy Valley – it would have been a long pull back up the hill for another go!

Below: The commons were also popular for tobogganing, for those who preferred gentler slopes. These tobogganers are enjoying themselves at Link Top; the Nag's Head and Link Terrace can be seen in the background.

Opposite above: Maypole dancing at Bromsberrow for the Coronation of King George V and Queen Mary in 1911.

Opposite below: Maypole dancers at Hanley Castle.

A horse-drawn charabanc outside the Three Horseshoes at Poolbrook. The licensee at the time was Edward Hughes, who was presumably one of the men in this picture.

A coach party from the Blue Bell on Guarlford Road setting off to the Shrewsbury Flower Show in 1936.

A dog show at Hanley Castle, *c.* 1910.

These young ladies at St Mary's, Hanley Swan are dressed as fisherwomen, complete with fish, in around 1910.

Above: A large crowd on Belle Vue Terrace, Easter 1907. The foxhounds are parading along the road.

Left: In the years prior to the First World War, Malvern Link held several Bicycle Carnivals. This man won first prize one year for constructing the Eiffel Tower on his bike, complete with drinking glasses and lemons on the front. Eiffel Tower was a popular maker of soft drinks at the time. This photograph was taken by Clem Walton.

Above: The entries at the 1914 Bicycle Carnival included a complete merry-go-round, what looks like a snowstorm, and an elephant with a lady rider in a houdah and with a mahout in attendance.

Right: This cyclist at the 1906 Carnival had a complete shop counter mounted on his bike.

Laying the foundation stone at Somers Park Methodist chapel, 1906.

Lady Barbara Yeatman-Biggs laying the foundation stone at Christchurch Parish Hall on 27 May 1905. The photograph was taken by Clem Walton of Court Road. The hall is now the auction room of Philip Serrell.

Lady Grey laying the foundation stone at Trinity Parish Hall on 19 September 1910.

Opposite below: The laying of the cornerstone at the Assembly Rooms on 26 July 1887. The photograph was taken by Norman May.

A 1913 motor club meeting on Malvern Link common, with Pickersleigh Road in the background. There are several three-wheeled Morgans in the foreground.

A photograph by Norman May of a group on a motor charabanc outing, *c.* 1915. It would have been a very bumpy ride with those solid tyres.

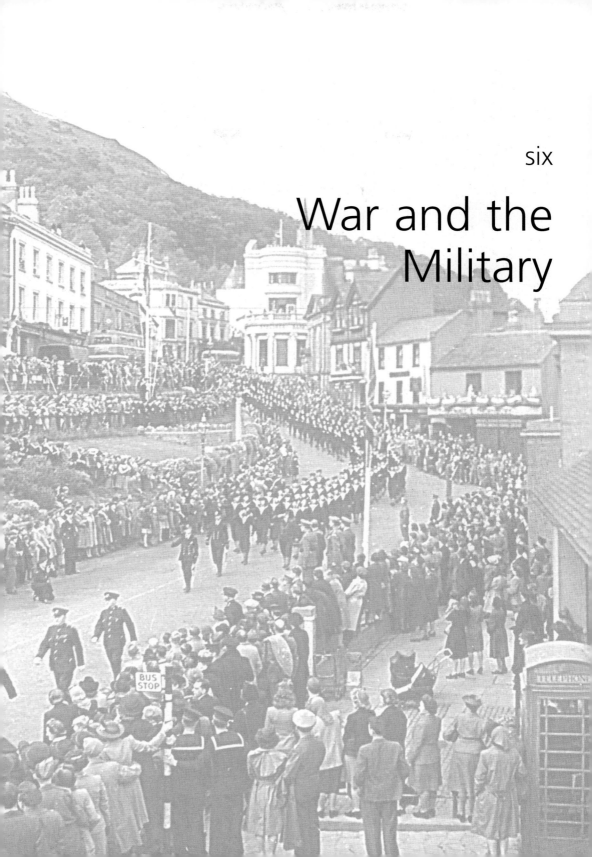

six

War and the Military

The 6th Gloucesters in camp at Malvern in 1914. Malvern was a popular site for military camps for various regiments from the surrounding counties. The soldiers in this photograph taken by Grosvenor are enjoying doorstep sandwiches, military pickle and slabs of fruitcake washed down with large mugs of tea.

Lloyd George, then Minister of Munitions, visiting the 13th Gloucester Regiment in camp at Malvern on 13 June 1915. Photograph by Clem Walton.

The old rural hospital in Hospital Bank found a new lease of life during the First World War as a military hospital, as this 1914 photograph shows. Note the varied assortment of regimental badges on the soldiers' caps.

Brand Lodge in Jubilee Drive was also used as a military hospital during the First World War. This ward looks very well appointed with its lace bedcovers and coal fire.

In 1916 Clem Walton took a series of photographs of a parade in Malvern to support the war effort, four of which are reproduced here. This float shows nurses of the Allied nations.

A float carrying soldiers in a trench. The poster asks, 'Why are you stopping here when your pals are out there?'

This bicycle–powered submarine has a sign on the side stating that 'Each recruit brings peace nearer'.

Another float in the parade, this time with a German Zeppelin flying over Navy ships.

Dad's Army – a platoon of the Home Guard at Malvern during the Second World War.

Staff and Wardens at the Malvern Laundry in Yates Hay Road, including Ralph Brown, Bert Edwards, Stella James, Dizzy Denman, Tom Burbeck, George Burbeck and Doris Rubery.

A parade in 1941 proceeding along Graham Road. The police and fire brigade seen here were joined by the ARP, nurses, the WVS and the Home Guard.

After the parade there was an inspection by Lord Dudley, accompanied by local dignitaries, in Priory Park.

Above: The Special Constabulary in Malvern in 1940. The uniform consisted of a cap, helmet, armband and whistle.

Left: Sea cadets march past at the VE Day celebrations. The crowd includes sailors from HMS *Duke* and American soldiers and Army nurses from the five American military hospitals based around Malvern. These hospitals provided 10,000 beds for war casualties.

Above: The visit to Malvern, on 9 July 1944, of King George VI and Queen Elizabeth. The King and Queen are being greeted by Lady Beauchamp and Major Kendall, chairman of Malvern Urban District Council. The man standing beside the King is A.P. Rowe of the Telecommunications Research Establishment (TRE).

Right: A parade on VE Day outside the general post office in Great Malvern.

Above: These are the boffins from the TRE during the Second World War. Much of the development of radar was done at Malvern, which prompted the comment, 'Waterloo was won on the playing fields of Eton but the Second World War was won on the playing fields of Malvern'.

Left: The crowd awaiting the VJ Day parade in Great Malvern. The car seems to have broken down and is being pushed away.

seven

Transport

Great Malvern station during the days of the Great Western Railway, with somewhat more staff than they have today. The station was designed by Elmslie and built in 1861. Unfortunately, the magnificent clock tower has long since disappeared.

Above: Tunnel Junction signal box. The signalman and trackside workers are posing for the camera, as is the child sat on the fence. The semaphore signals are still in use today. The telegraph wires on the poles alongside the track can be seen continuing over the top of the hills in the background.

Right: A Victorian photograph showing the construction of the railway tunnel and cutting under the hills, built by Stephen Ballard in 1856. The tunnel is 1,567 yards long at a gradient of 1:80. It was replaced by a new tunnel alongside in 1926, which was 1,589 yards long at a gradient of 1:90.

Opposite below: Great Malvern station, viewed from the road. The canopy sheltered passengers while they were entering or alighting from their carriages. The carriage with the white horse was a special cab used to transport visitors to and from various hotels in Malvern. The horse was called Mayday and his owner said that he was the 'best that ever came to Malvern. In six months he paid for himself in 1s and 2s fares'. Both the Great Western Railway and the Midland Railway operated from Great Malvern.

The Hanley Road LMS station at Malvern Wells, after its closure. The tracks and canopy have been removed and the scene looks very desolate. This line went to Ashchurch via Upton-on-Severn but it was closed in 1952.

A GWR pannier tank by the water tower at Malvern Wells.

A steam–hauled train coming under the Howsell Road bridge into Malvern Link station in the 1950s. The shed and sidings on the left were removed in the 1970s.

The cab which was used to transport visitors between the major hotels and Great Malvern station, seen outside the Portland Hotel in Church Street.

Carriages such as this one could by hired from various operators such as Edwin Trigg for journeys around the hills and the local area.

Edwin Trigg at the Unicorn also operated horse-drawn charabancs like this one, seen next to his booking office in Great Malvern in 1912. The board on the left advertises 'Drives for today: British Camp, Jubilee Drive, Round the Hills' and also offers services to West Malvern, Mathon, Cradley, Bosbury and Colwall.

eight

Schools

Wells House School, founded in 1860 by Dr William Gedge. This building had previously been one of the first water-cure establishments. The school closed in 1991 and today the buildings are in ruins.

The gymnasium at Wells House School.

Malvern has for many years been a centre of private education. These are the pupils of the Priory School in Church Street in 1912.

Lower Wyche School, *c.* 1910. Several of the boys have posies of flowers in their lapels.

Young girls, possibly pupils at North Malvern School, enjoying their break playing by the tank clock.

A group of West Malvern School pupils with their teachers, c. 1910.

A study by local photographers C. & E. Grosvenor of an unidentified group of local schoolgirls posing in fancy dress. They include pixies, shepherds, shepherdesses and hunters.

Pupils of a Colwall school in a 1925 photograph by A.H. Robbins of Malvern Link. These girls are holdings various items which presumably indicated skills that they were taught, including a plant, a floor mop, a money box, sports equipment, fruit, a handbell, musical instruments, a dinner gong and even a large box of Cadbury's chocolates.

Malvern Link School, after a fire in 1925. It is said that staff from the adjacent railway station assisted with removing the contents of the school to safety; some items can be seen piled up in the school grounds. The building was originally built as a railway hotel in 1867. During the Second World War, the tower was damaged by bombs dropped from a Luftwaffe aircraft. The school was eventually demolished in 1967 and replaced by a modern block of flats.

The Open Air School at West Malvern provided education for children suffering from TB. It is now a field study centre.

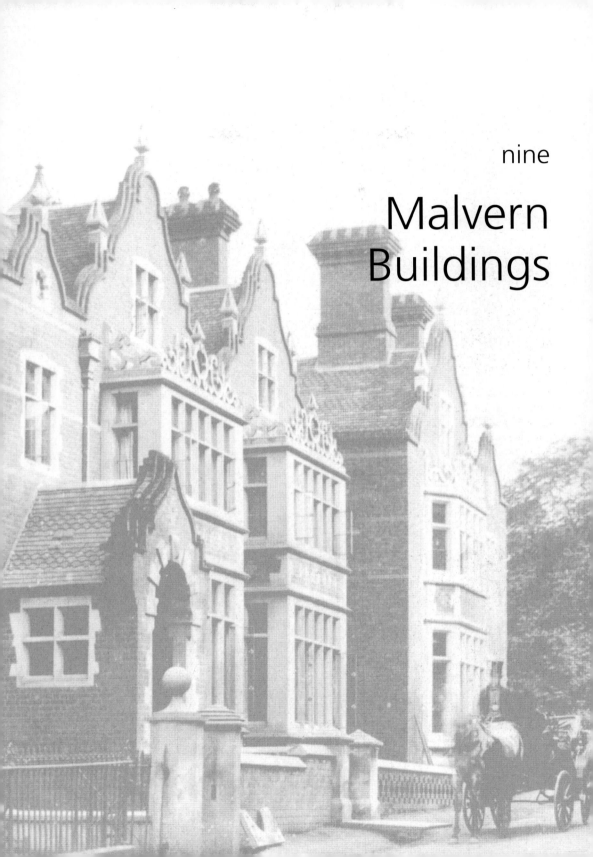

nine

Malvern
Buildings

An early
Victorian
carte de visite
photograph
of the Priory
Gatehouse in
around 1860.

The Priory Gatehouse, *c.* 1880. This was taken before the 1890s restoration, when the extension was added. There is a window and a door on the western elevation, from where A. Jenkins operated a shop selling game and vegetables. Two rabbits or hares can be seen hanging on a rail just to the right of the archway.

Right: This photograph, taken in around 1870, is entitled 'The Priory'. This indicates that it is a picture of the house of Dr Gully, which was later demolished and replaced by the present building, now the home of Malvern Hills District Council. Or it may be an early picture of the nearby Grange, in which case it has since undergone extensive exterior alterations.

Below: The Assembly Rooms in Grange Road were the forerunner of the Winter Gardens. Some of the buildings still exist today but the glass pavilion, then an art school, was demolished in the 1920s to make way for the Picture House.

A Victorian photograph of Pickersleigh House, which was looking rather overgrown at that time.

These cottages in Court Road stood next to the post office, which was then run by Alfred Green.

Above: This picturesque cottage was in Bond Street, off Howsell Road in Malvern Link and was the home of the Payter family. Photograph by C. & E. Grosvenor.

Right: The house at the Chalybeate Spa in Priory Road, *c.* 1880. The centre first-floor window is bricked in; it has since been reopened.

Foley House in Great Malvern. When this photograph was taken, Foley House was the home of the famous Marionette Theatre, owned and run by Waldo and Muriel Lanchester. The marionettes were often taken on tour, including a visit to Buckingham Palace to perform before the royal family. This was also the home of the St Ann's Pottery. Muriel Lanchester had previously studied under the famous potter Bernard Leach. One of the marionettes and examples of the pottery can be seen today in Malvern Museum.

This view of Trafalgar House, on Worcester Road in Great Malvern, cannot be seen today as an art deco extension of shops was added to the front in the 1920s. The fan-shaped tracery above the door is still visible in the entrance corridor, through the door between the Sue Ryder shop and the adjacent building society. The front elevation would have been similar to Foley House next door.

Right: Tudor House, *c.* 1880. This was once, with Holyrood House next door, the water–cure establishment of Dr Gully.

Below: The interior entrance hallway of Priory House, now the offices of Malvern Hills District Council.

Above: An early photograph, published by Henry Lamb of the Royal Library, of the original church at Newland.

Left: Hardwicke House, Abbey Road in the late nineteenth century, when it was the home of Dr Marsden. This fine building was left derelict for many years and was finally demolished in the 1960s and replaced with a modern block of apartments.

Holy Trinity church at Link Top, after its extensions were added. The entrance was originally on the other side.

The fondly remembered terrace of the Winter Gardens. Many local people and visitors, including famous actors during the Malvern festivals, enjoyed sitting here with a pot of tea and perhaps a cream cake.

Above: The Tyre Hill Inn at Hanley Swan. The proprietor, Mr W. Smith, could supply lunches, teas and cold snacks, as well as ales from Lewis Clarke's Worcester brewery.

Left: This windmill is thought to have been the one that stood at Wellington Heath. The photograph was taken by A.G. Allen of Colwall.

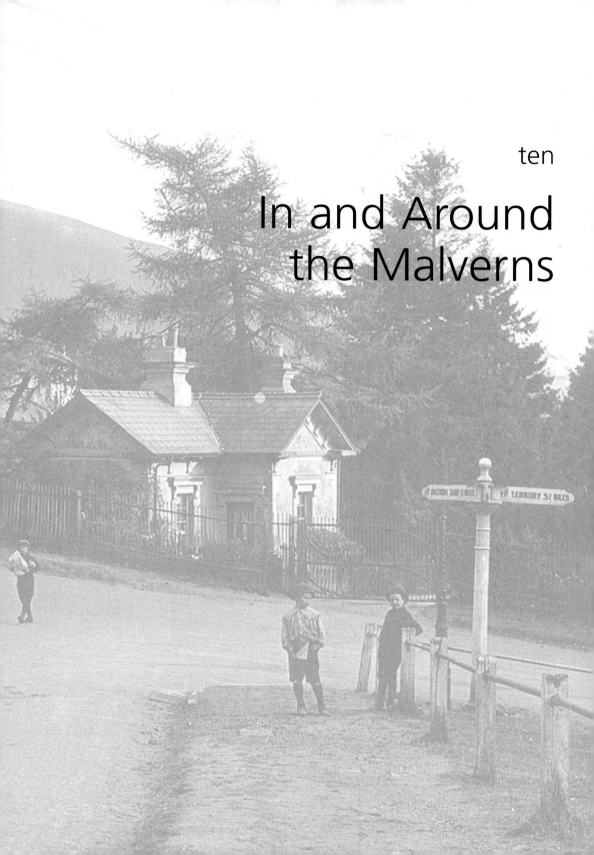

ten

In and Around
the Malverns

Above: The stocks, whipping post and pound on Kendalls Common on the North Malvern Road are all still there to this day.

Left: An early photograph of an overgrown tank clock tower in North Malvern before the later extension was added to the top.

The Promenade Gardens in Great Malvern, *c.* 1880. The ladies of the day preferred to sit in the shade to preserve their pale complexions.

The Promenade Gardens, looking in the opposite direction. The fountain can be seen on the left–hand side and Rose Bank beyond to the right.

Upper Colwall, *c.* 1915. The lady with the pram appears to have just had a dust shower from the speeding motorcycle. On the right, a lady is sitting on a pushchair while her young child plays alongside.

Malvern Wells, 1911. The Essington and Hornyold Arms Hotels can be seen in the middle distance but the general scene is more pastoral than it is nowadays.

Opposite below: The Colwall Park Hotel and Golf Club, with local lads and a horse and cart posing outside, *c.* 1910.

Locals posing outside the almshouses in Castlemorton at the beginning of the twentieth century. These buildings have survived.

Hanley Castle post office and stores in 1913. It was then kept by W. Tarling, who also produced this postcard. The poster between the windows says 'Recruits Wanted for Footguards', while the news of the day was 'Admiral Threatens to Resign'.

Hastings Pool at Barnards Green. The steam traction engine parked by the damaged railings was perhaps there to carry out repairs and was probably from the local council.

Above: Welland county police station. The posters are advertising 'Recruits Wanted at once for Reserve Regiments of the Yeomanry and 7th and 8th Battalions of Worcester Regiment for Service Abroad' and 'Keep the Flag Flying' and 'Join the Army Today and Serve the King'.

Right: The rose garden in Priory Park in the early 1950s. This was a peaceful, quiet area of the park where one could enjoy a little solitude.

Blackmore Park at Hanley Swan was the home of the Hornyold (Gandolfi) family. The house is no more but the entrance porch can still be seen today at Malvern Girls' College in Avenue Road. The site was used by the American Army during the Second World War as a military hospital.

Local children posing for the camera at Upper Colwall.

The Ledbury hounds at the British Camp on 5 March 1910.

Belle Vue Terrace, 1911.

Three biplane trainers that landed in field near Malvern Wells in 1942. Apparently one of the planes crashed while attempting to take off, luckily without any fatalities.

A close-up of one of the above Hawker aeroplanes.

Opposite below: Malvern Urban District Council obviously took publicity seriously in 1911.

Paddle boats on the pond in Priory Park in 1950. These boats, together with some Indian canoes were a popular feature for many years.

10.000
ILLUSTRATED GUIDES
DESPATCHED TO
600
URBAN DISTRICT COUNCILS
WITH INVITATION
TO HOLD THEIR CONFERENCE IN MALVERN
IN 1911.

Other local titles published by Tempus

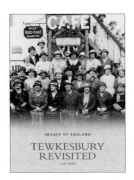

Tewkesbury Revisited

CLIFF BURD

This second selection of old photographs shows how Tewkesbury has developed from a vibrant trading post to one of the nation's favourite tourist places. With images of streets and businesses, as well as residents and visitors to the town, *Tewkesbury Revisited* will delight all those who have visited the area and wish to know more about its history, and will provide residents with a nostalgic look back into the past

0 7524 3476 4

Haunted Gloucester

EILEEN FRY AND ROSEMARY HARVEY

Gloucester's historic docks have some strange stories to tell and the city's twelfth-century cathedral also has its secrets. From a ghostly procession at Berkley Castle to the Grey Lady at the Theatre Royal, this new and fascinating collection of strange sightings and happenings in the city's streets, churches and public houses is sure to appeal to anyone intrigued by Gloucester's haunted heritage.

0 7524 3312 1

Motoring Around Hereford, Worcester & The Welsh Marches

A.B. DEMAUS

This richly illustrated volume on motoring in Hereford, Worcester and the Welsh Marches shows the many uses that wheeled transport has been put to. There are bicycles, cars of all shapes, sizes and ages, lorries, steam traction engines as well as views of motor sport in the area. Covered in detail are local manufacturers such as Morgan, now one of the largest independent motor manufacturers left in Britain.

0 7524 2361 4

Kidderminster: The Second Selection

ROBERT BARBER

This intriguing compilation of photographs provides a delightful insight into this Worcestershire town. The history of the town's great companies, both past and present, are explored including Brinton's Carpet Company, T. & A. Naylor, The Castle Motor Company, and the Sugar Factory which recently closed after seventy-seven years of production.

0 7524 2619 2

If you are interested in purchasing other books published by Tempus, or in case you have difficulty finding any Tempus books in your local bookshop, you can also place orders directly through our website

www.tempus-publishing.com